To Cheryl:

Happy

Love

Harold a Pat

D0292344

FEATURING THE ARTWORK OF

THOMAS KINKADE

OFF THE
Beaten Path

Publishers Since 1798

THOMAS NELSON PUBLISHERS®
a division of Thomas Nelson, Inc.

Nashville

Copyright © 2002 by Thomas Kinkade, Media Arts Group, Inc., Morgan Hill, CA

Published in Nashville, Tennessee, by Thomas Nelson, Inc.

Scripture references are from the following sources:

Scripture quotations noted NKJV are from THE NEW KING JAMES VERSION. Copyright © 1979, 1980, 1982, 1990, 1994, Thomas Nelson, Inc., Publishers.

Scripture quotations noted NIV are taken from the HOLY BIBLE, NEW INTERNATIONAL VERSION ®. Copyright © 1973, 1978, 1984 by International Bible Society. Used by permission of Zondervan Bible Publishing House. All rights reserved.

The "NIV" and "New International Version" trademarks are registered in the United States Patent and Trademark Office by International Bible Society. Use of either trademark requires the permission of International Bible Society.

Scripture quotations noted NCV are from the NEW CENTURY VERSION. Copyright © 1987, 1988, 1991 by Word Publishing, Nashville, Tennessee. Used by permission.

Scripture quotations noted KJV are from The Holy Bible, KING JAMES VERSION. Used by permission.

Produced with the assistance of The Livingstone Corporation. Project staff includes Katie E. Gieser, Paige Drygas, Jackie Sager, Janelle Poppe, and Ashley Taylor.

Design and production by: Que-Net Media™, Chicago

Library of Congress Cataloging-in-Publication Data

Kinkade, Thomas, 1958-
   Off the beaten path: devotional/Thomas Kinkade.
      p. cm.
   ISBN 0-7852-6573-2
     1. Devotional exercises. I. Title.
   BV4832.3 .K56 2001
   2242-dc21

Printed in the United States of America
02 03 04 05 06 QWV 7 6 5 4 3 2 1

Contents

Introduction

Each of us needs moments of quiet solitude,
when we can drift away from the frantic pace of everyday
life and wander off the beaten path. You're invited to
rest for a few moments within the pages of this book.
Step into the idyllic settings of Thomas Kinkade's
paintings. Set aside your agenda and your concerns,
and allow yourself to experience serenity.

As you immerse yourself in this peaceful world,
set your heart and your imagination free—free to
wander, to wonder, and to worship. In this collection,
you'll find selections of classic literature, poetry,
and Scripture, arranged in six thematic sections:
Wonder, Contemplation, Love, Solitude, Contentment,
and Grace. The uplifting words will elevate your spirit,
and as you notice the beauty of God's creation,
you'll be drawn into a sanctuary of repose.

Wonder

Little Women
Louisa May Alcott

Now and then, in this workaday world, things do happen in the delightful storybook fashion, and what a comfort that is. Half an hour after everyone had said they were so happy they could only hold one drop more, the drop came. Laurie opened the parlor door and popped his head in very quietly. He might just as well have turned a somersault and uttered an Indian war whoop, for his face was so full of suppressed excitement and his voice so treacherously joyful that everyone jumped up, though he only said, in a queer, breathless voice, "Here's another Christmas present for the March family."

Before the words were well out of his mouth, he was whisked away somehow, and in his place appeared a tall man, muffled up to the eyes, leaning on the arm of another tall man, who tried to say something and couldn't. Of course there was a general stampede, and for several minutes everybody seemed to lose their wits, for the strangest things were done, and no one said a word. Mr. March became invisible in the embrace of four pairs of loving arms; Jo disgraced herself by nearly fainting away, and had to be doctored by Laurie in the china closet; Mr. Brooke kissed Meg entirely by mistake, as he somewhat incoherently explained; and Amy, the dignified, tumbled over a stool, and, never stopping to get up, hugged and cried over her father's boots in the most touching manner.

That they should seek the Lord, if haply they might feel after him, and find him, though he be not far from every one of us: For in him we live, and move, and have our being; as certain also of your own poets have said, For we are also his offspring.
Acts 17:27–28 KJV

The Presence

Jones Very

I sit within my room and joy to find
That Thou who always loves art with me here,
That I am never left by Thee behind,
But by Thyself Thou keep'st me ever near;
The fire turns brighter when with Thee I look,
And seems a kinder servant sent to me;
With gladder heart I read Thy holy book,
Because Thou art the eyes by which I see;
This aged chair, that table, watch, and door
Around in ready service ever wait;
Nor can I ask of Thee a menial more
To fill the measure of my large estate,
For Thou Thyself, with all a Father's care,
Where'er I turns, art ever with me there.

Bliss

Katherine Mansfield

But in her bosom there was still that bright glowing place—that shower of little sparks coming from it. It was almost unbearable. She hardly dared to breathe for fear of fanning it higher, and yet she breathed deeply, deeply. She hardly dared to look into the cold mirror—but she did look, and it gave her back a woman, radiant, with smiling, trembling lips, with big, dark eyes and an air of listening, waiting for something . . . divine to happen . . . that she knew must happen . . . infallibly.

The Sound of the Sea

Henry Wadsworth Longfellow

The sea awoke at midnight from its sleep,
   And round the pebbly beaches far and wide
   I heard the first wave of the rising tide
   Rush onward with uninterrupted sweep;
A voice out of the silence of the deep,
   A sound mysteriously multiplied
   As of a cataract from the mountain's side,
   Or roar of winds upon a wooded steep.
So comes to us at times, from the unknown
   And inaccessible solitudes of being,
   The rushing of the sea-tides of the soul;
And inspirations, that we deem our own,
   Are some divine foreshadowing and foreseeing
   Of things beyond our reason or control.

The Lord is your keeper;
The Lord is your shade at your right hand.
The sun shall not strike you by day,
Nor the moon by night.
The Lord shall preserve you from all evil;
He shall preserve your soul.
The Lord shall preserve your going out and your coming in
From this time forth, and even forevermore.
Psalm 121:5–8 *NKJV*

A White Heron

Sarah Orne Jewett

The sparrows and robins in the woods below were beginning to wake and twitter to the dawn, yet it seemed much lighter there aloft in the pine-tree, and the child knew that she must hurry if her project were to be of any use.

The tree seemed to lengthen itself out as she went up, and to reach farther and farther upward. It was like a great main-mast to the voyaging earth; it must truly have been amazed that morning through all its ponderous frame as it felt this determined spark of human spirit winding its way from higher branch to branch. Who knows how steadily the least twigs held themselves to advantage this light, weak creature on her way! The old pine must have loved his new dependent. More than all the hawks, and bats, and moths, and even the sweet voiced thrushes, was the brave, beating heart of the solitary gray-eyed child. And the tree stood still and frowned away the winds that June morning while the dawn grew bright in the east.

A Cradle Song

William Blake

Sweet dreams form a shade,
O'er my lovely infants head.
Sweet dreams of pleasant streams,
By happy silent moony beams.

Sweet sleep with soft down,
Weave thy brows an infant crown.
Sweet sleep Angel mild,
Hover o'er my happy child.

Sweet smiles in the night,
Hover over my delight.
Sweet smiles Mothers smiles
All the livelong night beguiles.

Sweet moans, dovelike sighs,
Chase not slumber from thy eyes.
Sweet moans, sweeter smiles,
All the dovelike moans beguiles.

Sleep sleep happy child.
All creation slept and smil'd.
Sleep sleep, happy sleep,
While o'er thee thy mother weep.

Sweet babe in thy face,
Holy image I can trace.
Sweet babe once like thee,
Thy maker lay and wept for me

Wept for me for thee for all,
When he was an infant small.
Thou his image ever see,
Heavenly face that smiles on thee.

Smiles on thee on me on all,
Who become an infant small,
Infant smiles are his own smiles.
Heaven and earth to peace beguiles.

I will praise You, for I am fearfully and wonderfully made;
Marvelous are Your works,
And that my soul knows very well.
My frame was not hidden from You,
When I was made in secret,
And skillfully wrought in the lowest parts of the earth.
Your eyes saw my substance, being yet unformed.
And in Your book they all were written,
The days fashioned for me,
When as yet there were none of them.
Psalm 139:14–16 NKJV

The Picture of Dorian Gray

Oscar Wilde

The studio was filled with the rich odour of roses, and when the light summer wind stirred amidst the trees of the garden, there came through the open door the heavy scent of the lilac, or the more delicate perfume of the pink-flowering thorn.

From the corner of the divan of Persian saddle-bags on which he was lying, smoking, as was his custom, innumerable cigarettes, Lord Henry Wotton could just catch the gleam of the honey-sweet and honey-coloured blossoms of a laburnum, whose tremulous branches seemed hardly able to bear the burden of a beauty so flame-like as theirs; and now and then the fantastic shadows of birds in flight flitted across the long tussore-silk curtains that were stretched in front of the huge window, producing a kind of momentary Japanese effect, and making him think of those pallid jade-faced painters of Tokyo who, through the medium of an art that is necessarily immobile, seek to convey the sense of swiftness and motion.

The sullen murmur of the bees shouldering their way through the long unmown grass, or circling with monotonous insistence round the dusty gilt horns of the straggling woodbine, seemed to make the stillness more oppressive. The dim roar of London was like the bourdon note of a distant organ.

I am not saying this because I am in need, for I have learned to be content whatever the circumstances. I know what it is to be in need, and I know what it is to have plenty. I have learned the secret of being content in any and every situation, whether well fed or hungry, whether living in plenty or in want. I can do everything through him who gives me strength.
Philippians 4:11–13 NIV

The Country Life, to the Honored Endymion Porter...

Robert Herrick

Sweet country life, to such unknown,
Whose lives are others', not their own!
But, serving courts and cities, be
Less happy, less enjoying thee . . .
When now the cock, the plowman's horn,
Calls forth the lily-wrested morn,
Then to thy corn-fields thou dost go,
Which, though well soiled, yet thou dost know
That the best compost for the lands
Is the wise master's feet and hands.
There at the plow thou find'st thy team,
With a hind whistling there to them,
And cheer'st them up by singing how
The kingdom's portion is the plow . . .
O happy life! if that their good
The husbandmen but understood,
Who all the day themselves do please,
And younglings, with such sports as these;
And, lying down, have naught t'affright
Sweet sleep, that makes more short the night.

Thomas
Kinkade

Alice's Adventures in Wonderland

Lewis Carroll

Alice was beginning to get very tired of sitting by her sister on the bank, and of having nothing to do: once or twice she had peeped into the book her sister was reading, but it had no pictures or conversations in it, "and what is the use of a book," thought Alice, "without pictures or conversations?"

So she was considering in her own mind (as well as she could, for the hot day made her feel very sleepy and stupid) whether the pleasure of making a daisy-chain would be worth the trouble of getting up and picking the daisies, when suddenly a White Rabbit with pink eyes ran close by her.

There was nothing so *very* remarkable in that; nor did Alice think it so very much out of the way to hear the Rabbit say to itself, "Oh dear! Oh dear! I shall be too late!" (when she thought it over afterwards, it occurred to her that she ought to have wondered at this, but at the time it all seemed quite natural); but when the Rabbit actually *took a watch out of its waistcoat-pocket*, and looked at it, and then hurried on, Alice started to her feet, for it flashed across her

mind that she had never before seen a rabbit with either a waistcoat-pocket, or a watch to take out of it, and burning with curiosity, she ran across the field after it, and was just in time to see it pop down a large rabbit-hole under the hedge.

"Come to Me, all you who labor and are heavy laden, and I will give you rest. Take My yoke upon you and learn from Me, for I am gentle and lowly in heart, and you will find rest for your souls. For My yoke is easy and My burden is light."
Matthew 11:28–30 NKJV

She Walks in Beauty

George Gordon, Lord Byron I

I

She walks in Beauty, like the night
    Of cloudless climes and starry skies;
And all that's best of dark and bright
    Meet in her aspect and her eyes:
Thus mellow'd to that tender light
    Which Heaven to gaudy day denies.

II

One shade the more, one ray the less,
    Had half impair'd the nameless grace
Which waves in every raven tress,
    Or softly lightens o'er her face;
Where thoughts serenely sweet express
    How pure, how dear their dwelling-place.

III

And on that cheek, and o'er that brow,
    So soft, so calm, yet eloquent,
The smiles that win, the tints that glow,
    But tell of days in goodness spent,
A mind at peace with all below,
    A heart whose love is innocent!

Confessions

St. Augustine

But how didst Thou make the heaven and the
earth, and what was the tool of such a mighty work as
Thine? For it was not like a human worker fashioning
body from body, according to the fancy of his mind,
able somehow or other to impose on it a form which
the mind perceived in itself by its inner eye (yet how
should even he be able to do this, if Thou hadst not
made that mind?). He imposes the form on something
already existing and having some sort of being, such as
clay, or stone or wood or gold or such like (and where
would these things come from if Thou hadst not
furnished them?). For Thou madest his body for the
artisan, and Thou madest the mind which directs the
limbs; Thou madest the matter from which he makes
everything; Thou didst create the capacity by which he
understands his art and sees within his mind what he
may do with the things before him.

Pilgrim's Progress
John Bunyan

Behold, how these Crystal Streams do glide,
To comfort pilgrims by the highway side.
The meadows green, besides their fragrant smell,
Yield dainties for them; And he that can tell
What pleasant fruit, yes, leaves these trees do yield,
Will soon sell all, that he may buy this field.

And He went up on the mountain and called to Him
those He Himself Wanted. And they came to Him.
Mark 3:13 NKJV

Thomas
Kinkade

Contemplation

Pride and Prejudice
Jane Austen

Elizabeth, as they drove along, watched for the first appearance of Pemberley Woods with some perturbation; and when at length they turned in at the lodge, her spirits were in a high flutter.

The park was very large, and contained great variety of ground. They entered it in one of its lowest points, and drove for some time through a beautiful wood, stretching over a wide extent.

Elizabeth's mind was too full for conversation, but she saw and admired every remarkable spot and point of view. They gradually ascended for half a mile, and then found themselves at the top of a considerable eminence, where the wood ceased, and the eye was instantly caught by Pemberley House, situated on the opposite side of a valley into which the road with some abruptness wound. It was a large, handsome, stone building, standing well on rising ground, and backed by a ridge of high woody hills; and in front, a stream of some natural importance was swelled into greater, but without any artificial appearance. Its banks were neither formal nor falsely adorned. Elizabeth was

delighted. She had never seen a place for which nature had done more, or where natural beauty had been so little counteracted by an awkward taste. They were all of them warm in their admiration; and at that moment she felt that to be mistress of Pemberley might be something!

Bless the Lord, O my soul;
And all that is within me, bless His holy name!
Bless the Lord, O my soul,
And forget not all His benefits:
Who forgives all your iniquities,
Who heals all your diseases,
Who redeems your life from destruction,
Who crowns you with lovingkindness and tender mercies,
Who satisfies your mouth with good things,
So that your youth is renewed like the eagle's.
Psalm 103:1–5 NKJV

My Friends,
the Things That Do Attain

Henry Howard, Earl of Surrey

My friend, the things that do attain
The happy life be these, I find:
The riches left, not got with pain;
The fruitful ground; the quiet mind;

The equal friend; no grudge, no strife;
No charge of rule, nor governance;
Without disease, the healthy life;
The household of continuance;

The faithful wife, without debate;
Such sleeps as may beguile the night;
Content thyself with thine estate,
Neither wish death, nor fear his might.

37

Wuthering Heights

Emily Bronte

The ledge, where I placed my candle, had a few mildewed books piled up in one corner; and it was covered with writing scratched on the paint. This writing, however, was nothing but a name repeated in all kinds of characters, large and small—*Catherine Earnshaw*, here and there varied to *Catherine Heathcliff*, and then again to *Catherine Linton*.

. . . Catherine's library was select, and its state of dilapidation proved it to have been well used; though not altogether for a legitimate purpose: scarcely one chapter had escaped a pen-and-ink commentary—at least, the appearance of one—covering every morsel of blank that the printer had left. Some were detached sentences; other parts took the form of a regular diary, scrawled in an unformed childish hand. At the top of an extra page (quite a treasure, probably, when first lighted upon) I was greatly amused to behold an excellent caricature of my friend Joseph—rudely, yet powerfully sketched. An immediate interest kindled within for the unknown Catherine, and I began forthwith to decipher her faded hieroglyphics.

6111

George Linley

Tho' lost to sight, to memory dear
Thou ever wilt remain;
One only hope my heart can cheer, —
The hope to meet again.

Oh, fondly on the past I dwell,
And oft recall those hours
When, wandering down the shady dell,
We gathered the wild-flowers.

Yes, life then seemed one pure delight,
Tho' now each spot looks drear;
Yet tho' thy smile be lost to sight,
To memory thou art dear.

Oft in the tranquil hour of night,
    When stars illume the sky,
I gaze upon each orb of light,
    And wish that thou wert by.

I think upon that happy time,
    That time so fondly loved,
When last we heard the sweet bells chime,
    As thro' the fields we roved.

He who observes the day, observes it to the Lord; and he who does not observe the day, to the Lord he does not observe it. He who eats, eats to the Lord, for he gives God thanks; and he who does not eat, to the Lord he does not eat, and gives God thanks. For none of us lives to himself, and no one dies to himself. For if we live, we live to the Lord; and if we die, we die to the Lord. Therefore, whether we live or die, we are the Lord's.
Romans 14:6-8 NKJV

Portrait of a Lady

Henry James

She had carried away an image from her visit to
his hill-top which her subsequent knowledge of him
did nothing to efface and which put on for her a
particular harmony with other supposed and divined
things, histories within histories: the image of a quiet,
clever, sensitive, distinguished man, strolling on a
moss-grown terrace above the sweet Val d'Arno and
holding by the hand a little girl whose bell-like
clearness gave a new grace to childhood. The picture
had no flourishes, but she liked its lowness of tone and
the atmosphere of summer twilight that pervaded it. It
spoke of the kind of personal issue that touched her
most nearly; of the choice between objects, subjects,
contacts—what might she call them?—of a thin and
those of a rich association; of a lonely, studious life in
a lovely land; of an old sorrow that sometimes ached
to-day; of a feeling of pride that was perhaps
exaggerated, but that had an element of nobleness;
of care for beauty and perfection so natural and so
cultivated together that the career appeared to stretch
beneath it in the disposed vistas and with the ranges of

steps and terraces and fountains of a formal Italian garden—allowing only for arid places freshened by the natural dews of a quaint half-anxious, half-helpless fatherhood.

Finally, brethren, whatever things are true, whatever things are noble, whatever things are just, whatever things are pure, whatever things are lovely, whatever things are of good report, if there is any virtue and if there is anything praiseworthy—meditate on these things. The things which you learned and received and heard and saw in me, these do, and the God of peace will be with you.
Philippians 4:8–9 NKJV

The Apology

Ralph Waldo Emerson

Think me not unkind and rude,
That I walk alone in grove and glen;
I go to the god of the wood
To fetch his word to men.

Tax not my sloth that I
Fold my arms beside the brook;
Each cloud that floated in the sky
Writes a letter in my book.

Chide me not, laborious band,
For the idle flowers I brought;
Every aster in my hand
Goes home loaded with a thought.

There was never mystery
But 'tis figured in the flowers,
Was never secret history
But birds tell it in the bowers.

One harvest from thy field
Homeward brought the oxen strong;
A second crop thine acres yield,
Which I gather in a song.

Thomas
Kinkade

Thomas Kinkade

The Call of the Wild

Jack London

It was beautiful spring weather, but neither dogs
nor humans were aware of it. Each day the sun rose
earlier and set later. It was dawn by three in the
morning, and twilight lingered till nine at night.
The whole long day was a blaze of sunshine.
The ghostly winter silence had given way to the great
spring murmur of awakening life. This murmur arose
from all the land, fraught with the joy of living.
It came from the things that lived and moved again,
things which had been as dead and which had not
moved during the long months of frost. The sap was
rising in the pines. The willows and aspens were
bursting out in young buds. Shrubs and vines were
putting on fresh garbs of green. Crickets sang in the
nights, and in the days all manner of creeping,
crawling things rustled forth into the sun. Partridges
and woodpeckers were booming and knocking in the
forest. Squirrels were chattering, birds singing, and
overhead honked the wild-fowl driving up from the
south in cunning wedges that split the air.

From every slope came the trickle of running water, the music of unseen fountains. All things were thawing, bending, snapping. The Yukon was straining to break loose the ice that bound it down. It ate away from beneath; the sun ate from above. Air-holes formed, fissures sprang and spread apart, while thin sections of ice fell through bodily into the river.

Two are better than one,
Because they have a good reward for their labor.
For if they fall, one will lift up his companion.
But woe to him who is alone when he falls,
For he has no one to help him up.
Again, if two lie down together, they will keep warm;
But how can one be warm alone?
Ecclesiastes 4:9–11 NKJV

Love's Philosophy

Percy Bysshe Shelley

I

The fountains mingle with the river,
    And the rivers with the ocean;
The winds of heaven mix forever
    With a sweet emotion;
Nothing in the world is single;
    All things by a law divine
In one another's being mingle:
    Why not I with thine?

II

See the mountains kiss high heaven,
    And the waves clasp one another;
No sister flower would be forgiven
    If it disdained its brother;
And the sunlight clasps the earth,
    And the moonbeams kiss the sea:
What are all these kissings worth,
    If thou kiss not me?

Confessions

St. Augustine

Look around; there are the heaven and the earth. They cry aloud that they were made, for they change and vary. Whatever there is that has not been made, and yet has being, has nothing in it that was not there before. This having something not already existent is what it means to be changed and varied. Heaven and earth thus speak plainly that they did not make themselves: "We are, because we have been made; we did not exist before we came to be so that we could have made ourselves!" And the voice with which they speak is simply their visible presence. It was Thou, O Lord, who madest these things. Thou art beautiful; thus they are beautiful. Thou are good, thus they are good. Thou art; thus they are. But they are not as beautiful, nor as good, nor as truly real as Thou their Creator art. Compared with Thee, they are neither beautiful nor good, nor do they even exist. These things we know, thanks be to Thee. Yet our knowledge is ignorance when it is compared with Thy knowledge.

Morning and Evening

Charles Spurgeon

All I meet I find assists me
         In my path to heavenly joy:
Where, though trials now attend me,
         Trials never more annoy.
Blest there with a weight of glory,
         Still the path I'll never forget
But, exulting, cry, it led me
         To my blessed Savior's seat.

And at our gates are pleasant fruit, all manner new and olds.
Which I have laid up for you, my beloved."
Song of Soloman 7:13 NKJV

Love

Middlemarch

George Eliot

That silent colloquy was perhaps only the more
earnest because underneath and through it all there
was always the deep longing which had really
determined her to come to Lowick. The longing was
to see Will Ladislaw. She did not know any good that
could come of their meeting: she was helpless; her
hands had been tied from making up to him for any
unfairness in his lot. But her soul thirsted to see him.
How could it be otherwise? If a princess in the days of
enchantment had seen a four-footed creature from
among those which live in herds come to her once
and again with a human gaze which rested upon her
with choice and beseeching, what would she think of
in her journeying, what would she look for when the
herds passed her? Surely for the gaze which had found
her, and which she would know again. Life would be
no better than candlelight tinsel and daylight rubbish
if our spirits were not touched by what has been,
to issues of longing and constancy.

Sonnet 18

William Shakespeare

Shall I compare thee to a summer's day?
Thou art more lovely and more temperate:
Rough winds do shake the darling buds of May,
And summer's lease hath all too short a date:
Sometime too hot the eye of heaven shines,
And often is his gold complexion dimm'd,
And every fair from fair sometimes declines,
By chance or natures changing course untrimm'd:
But thy eternal summer shall not fade,
Nor lose possession of that fair thou owest,
Nor shall death brag thou wandrest in his shade,
When in eternal lines to time thou growest,

> *So long as men can breathe or eyes can see*
> *So long lives this, and this gives life to thee.*

Whoever does not love does not know God, because God is love. This is how God showed his love to us: He sent his one and only Son into the world so that we could have life through him. This is what real love is: It is not our love for God; it is God's love for us in sending his Son to be the way to take away our sins. Dear friends, if God loved us that much we also should love each other.
1 John 4:8–11 NCV

Emma

Jane Austen

She hoped they might now become friends again.
She thought it was time to make up. Making up
indeed would not do. *She* certainly had not been in
the wrong, and *he* would never own that he had.
Concession must be out of the question; but it was
time to appear to forget that they had ever quarrelled;
and she hoped it might rather assist the restoration of
friendship that when he came into the room she had
one of the children with her—the youngest, a nice
little girl about eight months old, who was now
making her first visit to Hartfield, and very happy to be
danced about in her aunt's arms. It did assist; for
though he began with grave looks and short questions,
he was soon led on to talk of them all in the usual
way, and to take the child out of her arms with all the
unceremoniousness of perfect amity. Emma felt they
were friends again; and the conviction giving her at
first great satisfaction and then a little sauciness, she
could not help saying as he was admiring the baby,
"What a comfort it is that we think alike about our

nephews and nieces. As to men and women, our opinions are sometimes very different; but with regard to these children, I observe we never disagree."

> "Let not your heart be troubled; you believe in God, believe also in Me. In My Father's house are many mansions; if it were not so, I would have told you. I go to prepare a place for you. And if I go and prepare a place for you, I will come again and receive you to Myself; that where I am, there you may be also."
> John 14:1–3 NKJV

God's Grandeur

Gerard Manley Hopkins

The world is charged with the grandeur of God.
It will flame out, like shining from shook foil;
It gathers to a greatness, like the ooze of oil
Crushed. Why do men then now not reck his rod?
Generations have trod, have trod, have trod;
And all is seared with trade; bleared, smeared with toil;
And wears man's smudge and shares man's smell: the soil
Is bare now, nor can foot feel, being shod

And for all this, nature is never spent;
There lives the dearest freshness deep down things;
And though the last lights off the black West went
Oh, morning, at the brown brink eastward, springs—
Because the Holy Ghost over the bent
World broods with warm breast and with ah! bright wings.

Jane Eyre

Charlotte Bronte

He put me off his knee, rose, and reverently lifting his hat from his brow, and bending his sightless eyes to the earth, he stood in mute devotion. Only the last words of the worship were audible—

"I thank my Maker, that, in the midst of judgement, He has remembered mercy. I humbly entreat my Redeemer to give me strength to lead henceforth a purer life than I have done hitherto!"

Then he stretched his hand out to be led. I took that dear hand, held it a moment to my lips, and then let it pass round my shoulder: being so much lower of stature than he, I served both for his prop and guide. We entered the wood, and wended homeward.

A Happy Life

Earl of Westmorland

That which creates a happy life
Is substance left, not gained by strife,
A fertile and a thankful mold,
A chimney always free from cold;
Never to be the client, or
But seldom times the counselor.
A mind content with what is fit,
Whose strength doth most consist in wit;
A body nothing prone to be
Sick; a prudent simplicity.
Such friends as of one's own rank are;
Homely fare, not sought from far;
The table without art's help spread;
A night in wine not buried,

Yet drowning cares; a bed that's blest

With true joy, chastity, and rest;

Such short, sweet slumber as may give

Less time to die in't, more to live:

Thine own estate whate'er commend,

And wish not for, nor fear thine end.

Yet this I call to mind
    and therefore I have hope:
Because of the Lord's great love we are not consumed,
    for his compassions never fail.
They are new every morning;
    great is your faithfulness.
I say to myself, "The Lord is my portion;
    therefore I will wait for him."
Lamentations 3:21–24 NIV

Madame Bovary

Gustave Flaubert

The moon, dark red and perfectly round, was just climbing above the horizon, beyond the meadows. It rose swiftly behind the poplars, whose branches partially hid it like a torn black curtain, then it appeared in all its elegant whiteness, lighting up the cloudless sky; finally, moving more slowly, it cast on the surface of the river a large patch of light which glittered like an infinity of stars; the silvery gleam seemed to writhe all the way to the bottom of the water like a headless serpent covered with luminous scales. It also resembled a monstrous candlestick with molten diamonds streaming down its sides. The soft night enveloped them; the spaces between the leaves of the trees were filled in with dark shadows. Emma, her eyes half closed, breathed in the cool breeze with deep sighs. Lost in reverie, they did not speak. The sweetness of earlier days returned to their hearts, as abundant and silent as the flowing river, soft as the fragrance of the lilacs, and it projected into their memories longer and more melancholy shadows than those cast on the grass by the motionless willows.

Often some prowling nocturnal animal, a hedgehog or a weasel, would rustle through the foliage, and occasionally they heard the sound of a ripe peach dropping from one of the trees along the wall.

The precepts of the Lord are right,
giving joy to the heart.
The commands of the Lord are radiant,
giving light to the eyes.
The fear of the Lord is pure,
enduring forever.
The ordinances of the Lord are sure
and altogether righteous.
They are more precious than gold,
than much pure gold;
they are sweeter than honey,
than honey from the comb.
Psalm 19:8–10 NIV

There is a Garden in Her Face

Thomas Campion

There is a garden in her face
Where roses and white lilies grow;
A heavenly paradise is that place
Wherein all pleasant fruits do flow.
There cherries grow which none may buy
Till "Cherry-ripe" themselves do cry.

Those cherries fairly do enclose
Of orient pearl a double row,
Which when her lovely laughter shows,
They look like rose-buds filled with snow;
Yet them nor peer prince can buy,
Till "Cherry-ripe" themselves do cry.

Her eyes like angels watch them still;
Her brows like bended bows do stand,
Threatening with piercing frowns to kill
All that attempt, with eye or hand
Those sacred cherries to come nigh
Till "Cherry-ripe" themselves do cry.

Romeo and Juliet

William Shakespeare

ROMEO

But, soft! what light through yonder
window breaks?
It is the east, and Juliet is the sun.
Arise, fair sun, and kill the envious moon,
Who is already sick and pale with grief
That thou, her maid, art far more fair than she.
Be not her maid, since she is envious;
Her vestal livery is but sick and green,
And none but fools do wear it; cast it off.
It is my lady, O, it is my love!
O, that she knew she were!
She speaks, yet she says nothing; what of that?
Her eye discourses; I will answer it.—
I am too bold, 'tis not to me she speaks.
Two of the fairest stars in all the heaven,
Having some business, do entreat her eyes
To twinkle in their spheres till they return.
What if her eyes were there, they in her head?

The brightness of her cheek would shame those stars,
As daylight doth a lamp; her eyes in heaven
Would through the airy region stream so bright
That birds would sing and think it were not night.
See, how she leans her cheek upon her hand!
O, that I were a glove upon that hand,
That I might touch that cheek!

He Wishes for the Cloths of Heaven

William Butler Yeats

Had I the heavens' embroidered cloths,
Enwrought with golden and silver light,
The blue and the dim and the dark cloths
Of night and light and the half-light,
I would spread the cloths under your feet:
But I, being poor, have only my dreams;
I have spread my dreams under your feet;
Tread softly because you tread on my dreams.

The Shulamite to Her Beloved

Set me as a seal upon your heart,
As a seal upon your arm;
For love is as strong as death,
Jealousy as cruel as the grave;
Its flames are flames of fire,
A most vehement flame.
Many waters cannot quench love,
Nor can the floods drown it.
If a man would give for love
All the wealth of his house,
It would be utterly despised.
Song of Solomon 8:6–7 NKJV

Thomas
Kinkade

Middlemarch

George Eliot

Every limit is a beginning as well as an ending.
Who can quit young lives after being long in company
with them, and not desire to know what befell them
in their after-years? For the fragment of a life,
however typical, is not the sample of an even web:
promises may not be kept, and an ardent outset may
be followed by declension; latent powers may find
their long-waited opportunity; a past error may urge a
grand retrieval.

Marriage, which has been the bourne of so many
narratives, is still a great beginning, as it was to Adam
and Eve, who kept their honeymoon in Eden, but had
their first little one among the thorns and thistles of
the wilderness. It is still the beginning of the home
epic—the gradual conquest or irremediable loss of
that complete union which makes the advancing
years a climax, and age the harvest of sweet memories
in common.

That Time of Year Thou Mayst in Me Behold

William Shakespeare

That time of year thou mayst in me behold
When yellow leaves, or none, or few, do hang
Upon those boughs which shake against the cold,
Bare ruin'd choirs, where late the sweet birds sang.
In me thou seest the twilight of such day
As after sunset fadeth in the west,
Which by and by black night doth take away,
Death's second self, that seals up all in rest.
In me thou seest the glowing of such fire,
That on the ashes of his youth doth lie,
As the deathbed whereon it must expire,
Consum'd with that which it was nourish'd by.
This thou perceiv'st, which makes thy love more strong,
To love that well which thou must leave ere long.

Therefore we do not lose heart. Though outwardly we are wasting away, yet inwardly we are being renewed day by day. For our light and momentary troubles are achieving for us an eternal glory that far outweighs them all. So we fix our eyes not on what is seen, but on what is unseen. For what is seen is temporary, but what is unseen is eternal.

2 Corinthians 4:16–18 NIV

Pride and Prejudice

Jane Austen

It is a truth universally acknowledged that a single man in possession of a good fortune must be in want of a wife.

However little known the feelings or views of such a man may be on his first entering a neighbourhood, this truth is so well fixed in the minds of the surrounding families that he is considered as the rightful property of some one or other of their daughters.

"My dear Mr. Bennet," said his lady to him one day, "have you heard that Netherfield Park is let at last?"

Mr. Bennet replied that he had not.

"But it is," returned she; "for Mrs. Long has just been here, and she told me all about it."

Mr. Bennet made no answer.

"Do not you want to know who has taken it?" cried his wife impatiently.

"*You* want to tell me, and I have no objection to hearing it."

This was invitation enough.

"Why, my dear, you must know, Mrs. Long says that Netherfield is taken by a young man of large fortune

from the north of England; that he came down on Monday in a chaise and four to see the place, and was so much delighted with it that he agreed with Mr. Morris immediately; that he is to take possession before Michaelmas, and some of his servants are to be in the house by the end of next week."

"What is his name?"

"Bingley."

"Is he married or single?"

"Oh! single, my dear, to be sure! A single man of large fortune; four or five thousand a year. What a fine thing for our girls!"

"How so? how can it affect them?"

"My dear Mr. Bennet," replied his wife, "how can you be so tiresome! You must know that I am thinking of his marrying one of them."

Husbands, love your wives, even as Christ also loved the church, and gave himself for it; That he might sanctify and cleanse it with the washing of water by the word, That he might present it to himself a glorious church, not having spot, or wrinkle, or any such thing; but that it should be holy and without blemish. So ought men to love their wives as their own bodies. He that loveth his wife loveth himself.
Ephesians 5:25–28 KJV

Ode on Solitude

Alexander Pope

Happy the man, whose wish and care
A few paternal acres bound,
Content to breathe his native air,
In his own ground.

Whose herds with milk, whose fields with bread,
Whose flocks supply him with attire,
Whose trees in summer yield him shade,
In winter fire.

Blest! who can unconcern'dly find
Hours, days, and years slide soft away,
In health of body, peace of mind,
Quiet by day,

Sound sleep by night; study and ease
Together mix'd; sweet recreation,
And innocence, which most does please,
With meditation.

Thus let me live, unseen, unknown;
Thus unlamented let me dye;
Steal from the world, and not a stone
Tell where I lye.

Thomas
Kinkade

Solitude

The Awakening

Kate Chopin

There was a garden out in the suburbs; a small, leafy corner, with a few green tables under the orange trees. An old cat slept all day on the stone step in the sun, and an old *mulatresse* slept her idle hours away in her chair at the open window, till some one happened to knock on one of the green tables. She had milk and cream cheese to sell, and bread and butter. There was no one who could make such excellent coffee or fry a chicken so golden brown as she.

The place was too modest to attract the attention of people of fashion, and so quiet as to have escaped the notice of those in search of pleasure and dissipation. Edna had discovered it accidentally one day when the high-board gate stood ajar. She caught sight of a little green table, blotched with the checkered sunlight that filtered through the quivering leaves overhead. Within she had found the slumbering *mulatresse*, the drowsy cat, and a glass of milk which reminded her of the milk she had tasted in Iberville.

She often stopped there during her perambulations; sometimes taking a book with her, and sitting an hour or two under the trees when she found the place deserted. Once or twice she took a quiet dinner there alone, having instructed Celestine beforehand to prepare no dinner at home. It was the last place in the city where she would have expected to meet any one she knew.

The Spirit searches all things, even the deep things of God. For who among men knows the thoughts of a man except the man's spirit within him? In the same way no one knows the thoughts of God except the Spirit of God.
1 Corinthians 2:9–11 NIV

1624

Emily Dickinson

Apparently with no surprise

To any happy Flower

The Frost beheads it at its play—

In accidental power—

The blonde Assassin passes on—

The Sun proceeds unmoved

To measure off another Day

For an Approving God.

However, as it is written:

"No eye has seen,

　no ear has heard,

no mind has conceived

　what God has prepared for those who love him"—

but God has revealed it to us by his Spirit.

Great Expectations

Charles Dickens

Ours was the marsh country, down by the river, within, as the river wound, twenty miles of the sea. My first most vivid and broad impression of the identity of things, seems to me to have been gained on a memorable raw afternoon towards evening. At such a time I found out for certain, that this bleak place overgrown with nettles was the churchyard; and that Philip Pirrip, late of this parish, and also Georgiana wife of the above, were dead and buried; and that Alexander, Bartholomew, Abraham, Tobias, and Roger, infant children of the aforesaid, were also dead and buried; and that the dark flat wilderness beyond the churchyard, intersected with dykes and mounds and gates, with scattered cattle feeding on it, was the marshes; and that the low leaden line beyond, was the river; and that the distant savage lair from which the wind was rushing, was the sea; and that the small bundle of shivers growing afraid of it all and beginning to cry, was Pip.

A Boat beneath a Sunny Sky

Lewis Carroll

A boat beneath a sunny sky,
Lingering onward dreamily
In an evening of July.

Children three that nestle near,
Eager eye and willing ear,
Pleased a simple tale to hear.

Long has paled that sunny sky:
Echoes fade and memories die:
Autumn frosts have slain July.

Still she haunts me, phantomwise,
Alice moving under skies
Never seen by waking eyes.

Children yet, the tale to hear,
Eager eye and willing ear,
Lovingly shall nestle near.

In a Wonderland they lie,
Dreaming as the days go by,
Dreaming as the summers die:

Ever drifting down the stream
Lingering in the golden dream
Life, what is it but a dream?

For this we say to you by the word of the Lord, that we who are alive and remain
until the coming of the Lord will by no means precede those who are asleep. For the
Lord Himself will descend from heaven with a shout, with the voice of an archangel,
and with the trumpet of God. And the dead in Christ will rise first. Then we who are
alive and remain shall be caught up together with them in the clouds to meet the
Lord in the air. And thus we shall always be with the Lord. Therefore comfort one
another with these words.
1 Thessalonians 4:15–18 NKJV

Thomas
Kinkade

The Adventures of Huckleberry Finn

Samuel Clemens

The sun was up so high when I waked that I
judged it was after eight o'clock. I laid there in the
grass and the cool shade thinking about things, and
feeling rested and ruther comfortable and satisfied.
I could see the sun out at one or two holes, but mostly
it was big trees all about, and gloomy in there amongst
them. There was freckled places on the ground where
the light sifted down through the leaves, and the
freckled places swapped about a little, showing there
was a little breeze up there. A couple of squirrels
set on a limb and jabbered at me very friendly.
I was powerful lazy and comfortable—I didn't want
to get up and cook breakfast.

Song of Myself 31
Walt Whitman

I believe a leaf of grass is no less than the journey-work of the stars,

And the pismire is equally perfect, and a grain of sand, and the egg of the wren,

And the tree-toad is a chef-d'œuvre for the highest,

And the running blackberry would adorn the parlors of heaven,

And the narrowest hinge in my hand puts to scorn all machinery,

And the cow crunching with depress'd head surpasses any statue,

And a mouse is miracle enough to stagger sextillions of infidels. . . .

> The heavens declare the glory of God;
>   the skies proclaim the work of his hands.
> Day after day they pour forth speech;
>   night after night they display knowledge.
> There is no speech or language
>   where their voice is not heard.
> Their voice goes out into all the earth,
>   their words to the ends of the world.
> In the heavens he has pitched a tent for the sun.
> Psalm 19:1–4 NIV

Thomas Kinkade

Madame Bovary
Gustave Flaubert

They walked back to Yonville along the river.
Its level sank in summer, widening its banks and
revealing the bottoms of the walls of the gardens,
each of which had a few steps leading down to the
water. It ran silently, swift and cold-looking; long thin
grass swayed with the current, like disheveled green
hair growing in its limpid depths. Here and there an
insect with delicate legs was crawling or sitting on a
water-lily leaf or the tip of a reed. Sunbeams pierced
the little blue bubbles which kept forming and
bursting on the ripples; branchless old willows
mirrored their gray bark in the water; the meadows
around them seemed empty. It was dinnertime on the
farms. As the young woman and her companion
walked along they heard nothing but the rhythm of
their footsteps on the dirt path, the words they were
saying to each other and the sound of her dress
rustling all around her.

The Flower

George Herbert

How fresh, O Lord, how sweet and clean
Are thy returns! ev'n as the flowers in spring;
   To which, besides their own demean,
The late-past frosts tributes of pleasure bring.
        Grief melts away
        Like snow in May,
   As if there were no such cold thing.

   Who would have thought my shrivell'd heart
Could have recover'd greenness? It was gone
   Quite under ground; as flowers depart
To see their mother-root, when they have blown;
        Where they together
        All the hard weather,
   Dead to the world, keep house unknown. . . .
And now in age I bud again,
After so many deaths I live and write;
   I once more smell the dew and rain,
And relish versing: O my only light,
        It cannot be
        That I am he
   On whom thy tempests fell all night.

These are thy wonders, Lord of love,
To make us see we are but flowers that glide:
  Which when we once can find and prove,
Thou hast a garden for us, where to bide.
      Who would be more,
        Swelling through store,
Forfeit their Paradise by their pride.

The Lord appeared to us in the past, saying:
  "I have loved you with an everlasting love;
    I have drawn you with loving-kindness.
  I will build you up again
    and you will be rebuilt, O Virgin Israel.
  Again you will take up your tambourines
    and go out to dance with the joyful.
  Again you will plant vineyards
    on the hills of Samaria;
    the farmers will plant them
    and enjoy their fruit."
Jeremiah 31:3–5 NIV

105

Contentment

The Adventures of Huckleberry Finn

Samuel Clemens

This second night we run between seven and eight hours, with a current that was making over four mile an hour. We catched fish, and talked, and we took a swim now and then to keep off sleepiness. It was kind of solemn, drifting down the big still river, laying on our backs looking up at the stars, and we didn't ever feel like talking loud, and it warn't often that we laughed, only a little kind of a low chuckle. We had mighty good weather, as a general thing, and nothing ever happened to us at all, that night, nor the next, nor the next.

Every night we passed towns, some of them away up on black hillsides, nothing but just a shiny bed of lights, not a house could you see. The fifth night we passed St. Louis, and it was like the whole world lit up. In St. Petersburg they used to say there was twenty or thirty thousand people in St. Louis, but I never believed it till I see that wonderful spread of lights at two o'clock that still night. There warn't a sound there; everybody was asleep.

I Wandered Lonely as a Cloud

William Wordsworth

I wandered lonely as a cloud
That floats on high o'er vales and hills,
When all at once I saw a crowd,
A host, of golden daffodils;
Beside the lake, beneath the trees,
Fluttering and dancing in the breeze.

Continuous as the stars that shine
And twinkle on the milky way,
They stretched in never-ending line
Along the margin of a bay:
Ten thousand saw I at a glance,
Tossing their heads in sprightly dance.

The waves beside them danced; but they
Out-did the sparkling waves in glee:
A poet could not but be gay,
In such a jocund company:
I gazed—and gazed—but little thought
What wealth the show to me had brought:

For oft, when on my couch I lie
In vacant or in pensive mood,
They flash upon that inward eye
Which is the bliss of solitude;
And then my heart with pleasure fills,
And dances with the daffodils.

Show us Your mercy, Lord,
And grant us Your salvation.
I will hear what God the Lord will speak,
For He will speak peace
To His people and to His saints;
But let them not turn back to folly.
Surely His salvation is near to those who fear Him,
That glory may dwell in our land.
Psalm 85:7–9 NKJV

Sense and Sensibility
Jane Austen

The whole country about them abounded in beautiful walks. The high downs which invited them from almost every window of the cottage to seek the exquisite enjoyment of air on their summits, were an happy alternative when the dirt of the valleys beneath shut up their superior beauties; and towards one of these hills did Marianne and Margaret one memorable morning direct their steps, attracted by the partial sunshine of a showery sky, and unable longer to bear the confinement which the settled rain of the two preceding days had occasioned. The weather was not tempting enough to draw the two others from their pencil and their book, in spite of Marianne's declaration that the day would be lastingly fair, and that every threatening cloud would be drawn off from their hills; and the two girls set off together.

Up-Hill
Christina Rossetti

Does the road wind up-hill all the way?
    Yes, to the very end.
Will the day's journey take the whole long day?
    From morn to night, my friend.

But is there for the night a resting-place?
    A roof for when the slow dark hours begin.
May not the darkness hide it from my face?
    You cannot miss that inn.

Shall I meet other wayfarers at night?
    Those who have gone before.
Then must I knock, or call when just in sight?
    They will not keep you standing at that door.

Shall I find comfort, travel-sore and weak?
Of labour you shall find the sum.
Will there be beds for me and all who seek?
Yea, beds for all who come.

Then I will sprinkle clean water on you, and you shall be clean; I will cleanse you from all your filthiness and from all your idols. I will give you a new heart and put a new spirit within you; I will take the heart of stone out of your flesh and give you a heart of flesh. I will put My Spirit within you and cause you to walk in My statutes, and you will keep My judgments and do them.
Ezekiel 36:25–27 NKJV

Les Misérables

Victor Hugo

He would sit upon a wooden bench leaning against a broken trellis and look at the stars through the irregular outlines of his fruit trees. This quarter of an acre of ground, so poorly cultivated, so cumbered with shed and ruins, was dear to him, and satisfied him.

What was more needed by this old man who divided the leisure hours of his life, where he had so little leisure, between gardening in the daytime, and contemplation at night? Was not this narrow enclosure, with the sky for a background, enough to enable him to adore God in his most beautiful as well as in his most sublime works? Indeed, is not that all, and what more can be desired? A little garden to walk, and immensity to reflect upon. At his feet something to cultivate and gather; above his head something to study and meditate upon: a few flowers on the earth, and all the stars in the sky.

Pied Beauty

Gerard Manley Hopkins

Glory be to God for dappled things—
　　For skies of couple-colour as a brinded cow;
　　　　For rose-moles all in stipple upon trout that swim;
Fresh-firecoal chestnut-falls; finches' wings;
　　Landscape plotted and pieced—fold, fallow, and plough;
　　　　And all trades, their gear and tackle and trim.
All things counter, original, spare, strange;
　　Whatever is fickle, freckled (who knows how?)
　　　　With swift, slow; sweet, sour; adazzle, dim;
He fathers-forth whose beauty is past change:
　　　　Praise him.

You alone are the Lord. You made the heavens, even the highest heavens, and all their starry host, the earth and all that is on it, the seas and all that is in them. You give life to everything, and the multitudes of heaven worship you.
Nehemiah 9:6 NIV

Kidnapped

Robert Louis Stevenson

Early as day comes in the beginning of July, it was
still dark when we reached our destination, a cleft in
the head of a great mountain, with a water running
through the midst, and upon the one hand a shallow
cave in a rock. Birches grew there in a thin, pretty
wood, which a little further on was changed into a
wood of pines. The burn was full of trout; the wood
of cushat-doves; on the open side of the mountain
beyond whaups would be always whistling,
and cuckoos were plentiful. From the mouth of the
cleft we looked down upon a part of Mamore, and
on the sealoch that divides that country from
Appin; and this from so great a height, as made it
my continual wonder and pleasure to sit and
behold them.

The name of the cleft was the Heugh of
Corrynakiegh; and although from its height and being
so near upon the sea, it was often beset with clouds,
yet it was on the whole a pleasant place, and the five
days we lived in it went happily.

A Hymn to God the Father

John Donne

I

Wilt thou forgive that sin where I begun,

    Which was my sin, though it were done before?

Wilt thou forgive that sin, through which I run,

    And do run still: though still I do deplore?

        When thou hast done, thou hast not done,

        For, I have more.

II

Wilt thou forgive that sin which I have won

    Others to sin? and, made my sin their door?

Wilt thou forgive that sin which I did shun

    A year, or two: but wallowed in, a score?

        When thou hast done, thou hast not done,

        For I have more.

III

I have a sin of fear, that when I have spun

My last thread, I shall perish on the shore;

But swear by thy self, that at my death thy son

Shall shine as he shines now, and heretofore;

And, having done that, thou hast done,

I fear no more.

It is God who arms me with strength,
And makes my way perfect.
He makes my feet like the feet of deer,
And sets me on my high places.
Psalm 18:32–33 NKJV

Thomas Kinkade

Grace

A Doll's House

Henrik Ibsen

HELMER

You try and get some rest, and set your mind at peace again, my frightened little song-bird. Have a good long sleep; you know you are safe and sound under my wing. What a nice, cosy little home we have here, Nora! Here you can find refuge. Here I shall hold you like a hunted dove I have rescued unscathed from the cruel talons of the hawk, and calm your poor beating heart. And that will come, gradually, Nora, believe me. Tomorrow you'll see everything quite differently. Soon everything will be just as it was before. You won't need me to keep on telling you I've forgiven you; you'll feel convinced of it in your own heart. You don't really imagine me ever thinking of turning you out, or even of reproaching you? Oh, a real man isn't made that way, you know, Nora. For a man, there's something indescribably moving and very satisfying in knowing that he has forgiven his wife—forgiven her, completely and genuinely, from the depths of his heart.

Song from
The Indian Emperor

John Dryden

I

Ah fading joy, how quickly art thou past!
　　Yet we thy ruin haste.
As if the cares of human life were few,
　　We seek out new:
And follow fate, which would too fast pursue.

II

See how on every bough the birds express
　　In their sweet notes their happiness.
　　They all enjoy, and nothing spare;
　　But on their mother Nature lay their care:
Why then should man, the lord of all below,
　　Such troubles choose to know,
As none of all his subjects undergo?

III

Hark, hark, the waters fall, fall, fall,
And with a murmuring sound
Dash, dash upon the ground,
     To gentle slumbers call.

So let us be thankful, because we have a kingdom that cannot
be shaken. We should worship God in a way that pleases him
with respect and fear.
Hebrews 12:28 NCV

A Simple Heart

Gustave Flaubert

Then she wept as she listened to the story of the Passion. Why had they crucified Him, when He loved children, fed the multitudes, healed the blind, and had chosen out of humility to be born among the poor, on the litter of a stable? The sowing of the seed, the reaping of the harvest, the pressing of the grapes— all those familiar things of which the Gospels speak had their place in her life. God had sanctified them in passing, so that she loved the lambs more tenderly for love of the Lamb of God, and the doves for the sake of the Holy Ghost.

She found it difficult, however, to imagine what the Holy Ghost looked like, for it was not just a bird but a fire as well, and sometimes a breath. She wondered whether that was its light she had seen flitting about the edge of the marshes at night, whether that was its breath she had felt driving the clouds across the sky, whether that was its voice she had heard in the sweet music of the bells. And she sat in silent adoration, delighting in the coolness of the walls and the quiet of the church.

The Lamb

William Blake

Little Lamb, who made thee?
  Dost thou know who made thee?
Gave thee life, and bid thee feed,
By the stream and o'er the mead;
Give thee clothing of delight,
Softest clothing, wooly, bright:
Gave thee such a tender voice,
Making all the vales rejoice!
  Little Lamb, who made thee?
  Dost thou know who made thee?

Little Lamb, I'll tell thee,
Little Lamb, I'll tell thee!
He is calléd by thy name,
For he calls himself a Lamb:
He is meek, and he is mild,
He became a little child:
I a child, and thou a lamb,
We are calléd by his name.
Little Lamb, God bless thee.
Little Lamb, God bless thee.

But with the precious blood of Christ, who was like a pure and perfect lamb.
Christ was chosen before the world was made, but he was shown to the world in
these last times for your sake. Through Christ you believe in God, who raised
Christ from the dead and gave him glory. So your faith and your hope are in God.
1 Peter 1:19–21 NCV

Pilgrim's Progress
John Bunyan

Then I saw in my dream that Christian was as in a muse a while; to whom also Hopeful added this word, "Be of good cheer, Jesus Christ maketh thee whole." And with that, Christian brake out with a loud voice, "Oh I see him again! And he tells me, *When thou passest through the waters, I will be with thee, and through the rivers, they shall not overflow thee.*" Then they both took courage, and the enemy was after that as still as a stone, until they were gone over. Christian therefore presently found ground to stand upon; and so it followed that the rest of the River was but shallow. Thus they got over. Now upon the bank of the River, on the other side, they saw the two shining men again who there waited for them. Wherefore being come up out of the river they saluted them, saying, "We are ministering Spirits, sent forth to minister for those that shall be heirs of salvation." Thus they went along towards the Gate; now you must note that the City stood upon a mighty hill, but the pilgrims went up that hill with ease, because they had these two men to lead them up by the arms; also they

had left their mortal garments behind them in the River: for though they went in with them, they came out without them. They therefore went up here with much agility and speed, though the foundation upon which the City was framed was higher than the clouds. They therefore went up through the regions of the air, sweetly talking as they went, being comforted because they safely got over the River, and had such glorious companions to attend them.

That if you confess with your mouth the Lord Jesus and believe in your heart that God has raised Him from the dead, you will be saved. For with the heart one believes unto righteousness, and with the mouth confession is made unto salvation. Romans 10:9–10 NKJV

Love (III)
George Herbert

Love bade me welcome: yet my soul drew back,
    Guilty of dust and sin.
But quick-ey'd Love, observing me grow slack
    From my first entrance in,
Drew nearer to me, sweetly questioning,
    If I lack'd anything

A guest, I answer'd, worthy to be here:
    Love said, You shall be he.
I the unkind, ungrateful? Ah my dear,
    I cannot look on thee.
Love took my hand, and smiling did reply,
    Who made the eyes but I?

Truth Lord, but I have marr'd them: let my shame
    Go where it doth deserve.
And know you not, says Love, who bore the blame?
    My dear, then I will serve.
You must sit down, says Love, and taste my meat:
    So I did sit and eat.

Little Women
Louisa May Alcott

They would have been still more amazed if they
had seen what Beth did afterward. If you will believe
me, she went and knocked at the study door before
she gave herself time to think, and when a gruff voice
called out, "Come in!" she did go in, right up to
Mr. Laurence, who looked quite taken aback, and
held out her hand, saying, with only a small quaver in
her voice, "I came to thank you, sir, for—" But she
didn't finish; for he looked so friendly that she forgot
her speech and, only remembering that he had lost
the little girl he loved, she put both arms round his
neck and kissed him.

If the roof of the house had suddenly flown off,
the old gentleman wouldn't have been more
astonished; but he liked it,—oh, dear, yes, he liked it
amazingly!—and was so touched and pleased by that
confiding little kiss that all his crustiness vanished;
and he just set her on his knee, and laid his wrinkled
cheek against her rosy one, feeling as if he had got his
own little granddaughter back again. Beth ceased to
fear him from that moment, and sat there talking to

him as cozily as if she had known him all her life, for love casts out
fear, and gratitude can conquer pride. When she went home,
he walked with her to her own gate, shook hands cordially,
and touched his hat as he marched back again, looking very stately
and erect, like a handsome, soldierly old gentleman, as he was.

*There is no fear in love. But perfect love drives out fear, because fear has to do
with punishment. The one who fears is not made perfect in love.
We love because he first loved us. If anyone says, "I love God," yet hates his
brother, he is a liar. For anyone who does not love his brother, whom he has
seen, cannot love God, whom he has not seen. And he has given us this
command: Whoever loves God must also love his brother.*
1 John 4:18–21 NIV

I Sing the Body Electric
Walt Whitman

I have perceiv'd that to be with those I like is enough,
To stop in company with the rest at evening is enough,
To be surrounded by beautiful, curious, breathing, laughing flesh is enough,
To pass among them or touch any one, or rest my arm ever so lightly round his
or her neck for a moment, what is this then?
I do not ask any more delight, I swim in it as in a sea.

There is something in staying close to men and women and looking on them,
and in the contact and odor of them, that pleases the soul well,
All things please the soul, but these please the soul well.

Bibliography

1. Alcott, Louisa May. Little Women. New York: Collier/Macmillan, 1962.

2. Austen, Jane. Emma. New York: Penguin, 1996.

3. Austen, Jane. Pride and Prejudice. New York: Amsco School, 1989.

4. Austen, Jane. Sense and Sensibility. New York: Alfred A. Knopf, 1906.

5. Bronte, Charlotte. Jane Eyre. London: Penguin, 1985.

6. Bronte, Emily. Wuthering Heights. New York: Scholastic, 1961.

7. Bunyan, John. Pilgrim's Progress. New York: Penguin, 1987.

8. Carroll, Lewis. Alice's Adventures in Wonderland. New York: Viking, 1975.

9. Chopin, Kate. "The Awakening, XXXVI."
   The Norton Anthology of Literature by Women. 2nd Edition.
   New York: W.W. Norton and Company, 1996.

10. Clemens, Samuel. "The Adventures of Huckleberry Finn."
    The Norton Anthology of American Literature. 4th Edition, Vol. 2.
    New York: W.W. Norton and Company, 1994.

11. Dickens, Charles. Great Expectations. London: Penguin, 1965.

12. Eliot, George. Middlemarch. New York: W. W. Norton, 1977.

13. Flaubert, Gustave. Madame Bovary. New York: Bantam, 1989.

14. Hugo, Victor. Les Misérables. New York: Washington Square, 1964.

15. Ibsen, Henrik. "A Doll's House." Four Major Plays.
    New York: Oxford University, 1981.

16. James, Henry. Portrait of a Lady. New York: W. W. Norton, 1995.

17. London, Jack. The Call of the Wild and Other Stories.
    Cornwall, NY: Cornwall, 1960.

18. Mansfield, Katherine. "Bliss." The Story and Its Writer. 5th Edition.
    Ed. Ann Charters. Boston: Bedford/St. Martins, 1999.

19. Shakespeare, William. Romeo and Juliet.: Logan, IA: Perfection Form, 1985.

20. Spurgeon, Charles H. Morning and Evening. Nashville:
    Thomas Nelson Pubishers, 1994.

21. Stevenson, Robert Louis. Kidnapped. London: Penguin, 1994.

22. St. Augustine. Confessions. Nashville: Thomas Nelson Publishers, 1999.

23. Wilde, Oscar. The Picture of Dorian Gray. New York: Modern Library, 1998.

Artwork used in
Off the Beaten Path
includes:

WONDER

Deer Creek Cottage, Christmas Cottage VI

Beacon of Hope, Seaside Memories I

Sweetheart Cottages III

The Miller's Cottage, Thomashire

Cottage by the Sea

The Mountains Declare His Glory

CONTEMPLATION

Gardens Beyond Autumn Gate

Glory of Winter

The Open Gate, Summer Gate II

Evening Glow

Morning Dogwood

LOVE

Autumn Lane

Lake Side Hideaway

Mountain Majesty, Beginning of a Perfect Day III

Beside Still Waters, Streams of Living Water I

Hidden Arbor, Secret Garden Places II

Autumn at Ashley's Cottage, Sugar and Spice Cottages II

Everett's Cottage

Artwork used in
Off the Beaten Path
includes:

SOLITUDE

Hidden Cottage II

Emerald Isle Cottage

The Mountains Declare His Glory

The Garden of Promise

CONTENTMENT

Blessings of the Summer, Blessings of the Seasons III

Spring in the Alps

Stillwater Bridge

Dusk in the Valley

GRACE

Morning Dogwood

Sunrise, A Prayer of Hope for the New Millennium of Light

Winter's End

Chapels of Nature